Sonia Bueno was born in the Spanish North African enclave of Melilla in 1976. She has published two collections of poetry: *retales* (*leftovers*, which won the Premio Internacional de Poesía Fundación Centro de Poesía José Hierro in 2011) and *Aral* (2016). Her poems have appeared in literary magazines in Spain and abroad, including the English-language magazine *The Wolf*. She was an invited reader at the 49th Rotterdam Poetry International in 2018. She lives in Madrid.

ARAL

ARAL

POEMS BY SONIA BUENO

ILLUSTRATIONS BY EUGENIA CRIADO
TRANSLATED BY JAMES WOMACK

This book was first published as *Aral* in 2016 by Amargord Ediciones in Madrid (Spain)

Text © Sonia Bueno 2016
Translation © James Womack 2019
Images © Eugenia Criado 2016

Cover design © Zuri Negrín 2019
This edition © Nevsky Editions, Ltd, 2019

http://calquepress.com
ISBN: 978 1 9162321 1 2
Type: Hoefler Text

British Library Cataloguing-in-Publication Data
A catalogue record for this book is available from the British Library

Calque Press
An imprint of Nevsky Editions Ltd.
2019

This book has been printed in the EU on paper produced from certified sustainable sources.

ARAL

with Rafa Calleja
We found the stairs by touch
Bruno Schulz

PHOTO[N]GRAPH I

harrowed   light.

bright

gall.

*heaven-blue
stone*

new   dyed.

aral   light.

a dry

saffron   eye.

II SHIPWRECKS IN A KNOT
OR
MISCELLANY
BY WAY OF A PROLOGUE

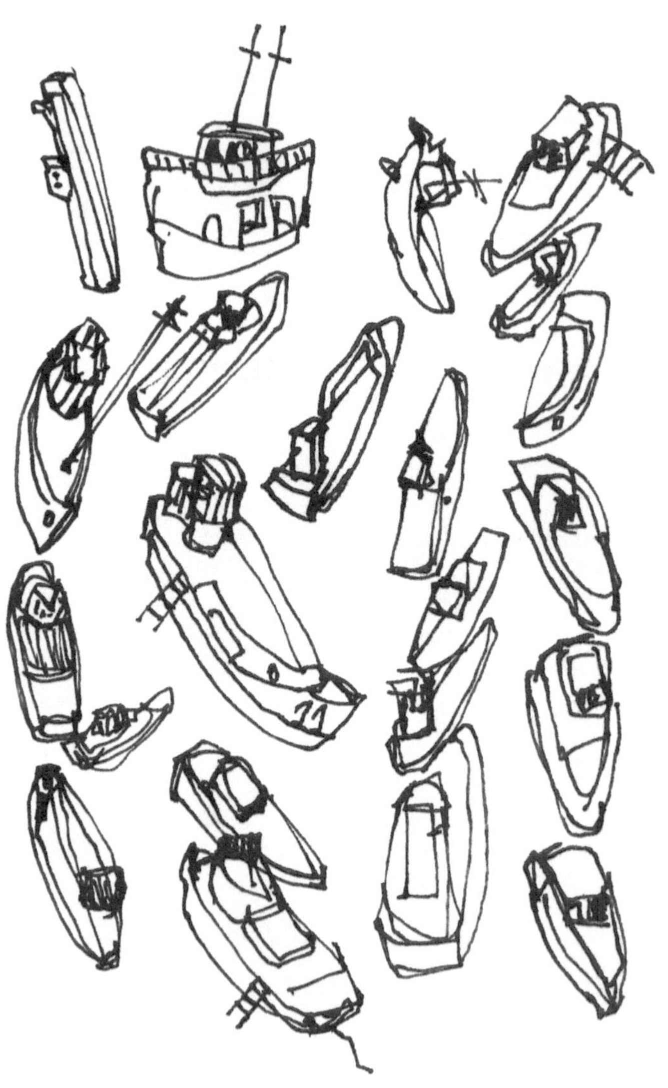

a burnt *cove* a story breaking under our feet a "speak of
customs as silence would speak"   a dawn torn almost
by memory those signs
s c a l e s
          decay even their name *mast*ername is gone
because the wind yes

and in the decay what listens will prosper   an arrow in
the white margins.

to walk into the empty sea. to stroke. that which dries
the word. to grub through the sea. the emptied sea. like an
image. to grub through the seabed. and not to speak

Lara Notebook I

like water invasive absence occupies the dust its house
piles up scabs with no skin suffixes with no root *sou/veneers*
with no image images that do not overflow and anyhow
rock like a seed asleep

sulphur city inside a yellow fishtank all the more fishtank
with no water sweat only the eyelid "only sweat to quench
our thirst" city lived by sulphur eyes look from the fish
tank the huddled seekers of other dry eyes look stranger
when they sight you don't know if they look or appear

[

     no hook no leaf lives on of the fisherman

     glass the dust in the eye when it hesitates

                     ]

Nukus, 6 August, Lara Notebook I

to embra*haze*

       the scar

           :   a bridge of bone

       sperm

dust

sight the poem {how it scabs over / the chance of sewing
wings on a bird / and / vanishing (like that!) / in the stitches}

nest (lest)
        knots (last)
                nets (least)

(en)compass

and
go down
anew

from the silent horizon
to the horizon from wall to another
from a self itself identical the fish
falls from its name if the spring's
flow's cut.

      —untalking of

altar desert(ed) sea worked down to the size
of the chalice

"while the gods march to their sacrifice
the fish
            twists hookshaped

and polish it with mud mirror of everything mirror
and to persevere in the task / to grow distant
as they do

a wall with no words a wall still more wall
more written
                guides us

if a word gets *close* then it is right to say it —otherwise
frame the word on a wall in the Nukus Museum
where it goes into death with *other*

                             things

Lara Notebook I

the deadliest   part of language —t h i s

be quiet   or don't be quiet

: no ^{truths} but in things

but things are

in this thing called language

THE PICKLE FACTORY
OR
NOTEBOOK OF EMPTIED THINGS
OR HOW TO GET RID OF COMMAS AND
BRACKETS
ITALICS *NEVER* PERFORM
WITHOUT CHANGING THE CONTENT

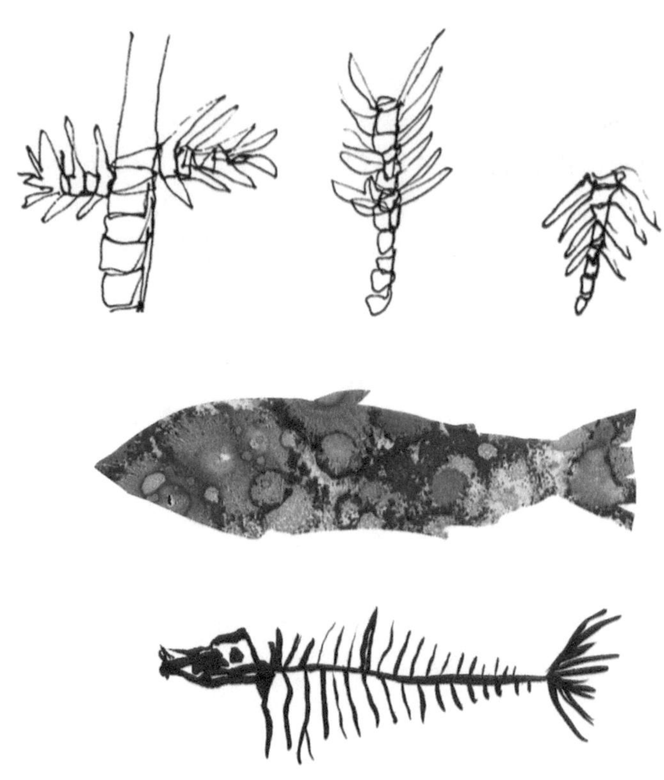

when he strains his ears he feels his body under a skin of
open eyes these sounds winnowed all mix with the dark
ness and in the mixture a syllable crackles   *one asks then if*
this capacity you have to set gears moving   separates them

          it bites like little roots
it nurtures itself on words things
          until the last wordt hing(e)s on a wordt hing(e)

          by the frame of reference an
automatic   contractionandwithdrawal

because it knows that *all forget themselves*
                         "appetite breeds milk from sand

in a circle move   it boycotts or blocks or grasps *oh*
demon of choice its own footprints   in a circle
centre as close to the rim   or   p u t it better
un centre   whatever   it   lies

a broke bottomed chalice
wing in negative as though the centre mirrored
most mirrored swings round the hand that does not
know itself

although the hand plots belief untying   vowels
in the darkness
silence doesn't extend doesn't f o l l o w the swing
                                        does not seduce
lines into whiteness

                                    it   bites them

        hardmarks night

/ as all the / cans / are the same it prefers to chew labels
/ un stuck from / papers ad here to the palate / words
swell its / mouth   / the collage of
tongues swallowed sur*prizes* / the naked / knotted
corpses /

                fishbone
goldsmith   vacuum
packs language far from
language   of the
                vacuum

the word
recognises it is used
up by over winding or carding
wound in the fact   ory it's more
a hermetic   closure
and bolus   lie
inside   each
tin lovely   for the tongue very very sweet
recognises that from time to
time it is recognised a
stone *feels*
hardness

:

can tin badge preserve   *weary*   c a c h e
of fishbones like so many words or
as if in eating them there were no
deceit or as though a can were a last of
feathers

:

although all left in the factory is the hand's s
wing *to see* what can't be said reach the secret gear
that gives the exact [whatever] of the name

that which we don't know and
barely suspect

written outside the factory outside the book it we(h)aves
a net
of f[r]ictions stains morningness   a hand no one reads
when   it   turns   on   the   light   closes   the   latch
let nothing write
if it traces out before the text or just shines   "to brick
the factory door shut with *all the knots* inside

LARA NOTEBOOK II

it bows down to the
                        flame
—and sows leaves
all around

(wind plays
                        at not b e i n g
the wind or does not play   )

                     in one face
the emptiness illuminates

in *the* other—

because the word is an eye they walk in silence
/ they are all ribs
/ they fill with signs / separate ly

they climb

                                                another's
                                        body
                                with
                        all the
                ballast
        of their
bodies

there
is
a
truth
here
:
there
is
something
loves
the
ladder

its
descent

it sews *its own* feet

it embroiders a ring
in *its* cheek

it doesn't distinguish between skins it shares a shroud

and [ameneedle]
calls

communion

their bodies *are* filled
with light   but another
hand is
the one which scatters seeds
for
   the fire

beyond the night
they plough the night
guided by the
boatman
                    and a lamp
of distant stars

a space {the river thirst's mirror / broken / moving
un / expectedly / they recognise each other but who /
                              drinks / from a mirage}

after many nights they real
lies

—come home on the first night or
                on the night before

the only (w/l)ord—

                [his skin has moth
he knows that *this torment* is the echo   of scales]

the place they travel to *the place* they retrace years ago
their feet have dried the sea and they still track
complete waves

—another   scrabbles in the horizon of thirst

even his nails describe
                                a yellow
                                        mutter

                                                as though of waves
                        other splintered nails

season by season the debris dismembers its memory

after each season another season required to undertake
        / the bone journey

the brightness
                        before the maps burn

footprint breaks another footprint
shapes *the sound*

                          "these heartbeats

                                    the calque

                        of another voice

don't blink don't stop don't
bend over   —whoever quits will wash his eyes
with dormant
            butterflies

to insist
as you walk on sipping the thread
you drew tight its
                    f
                    r
                    a
                    g
                    i
                    l
                    i
                    t
                    y

acid *if it is hung*

"action they desire: to try different shapes of tiredness
to fly above night time pathways

FOR AN UNFINISHED EPILOGUE
WRITTEN AS A HINGE

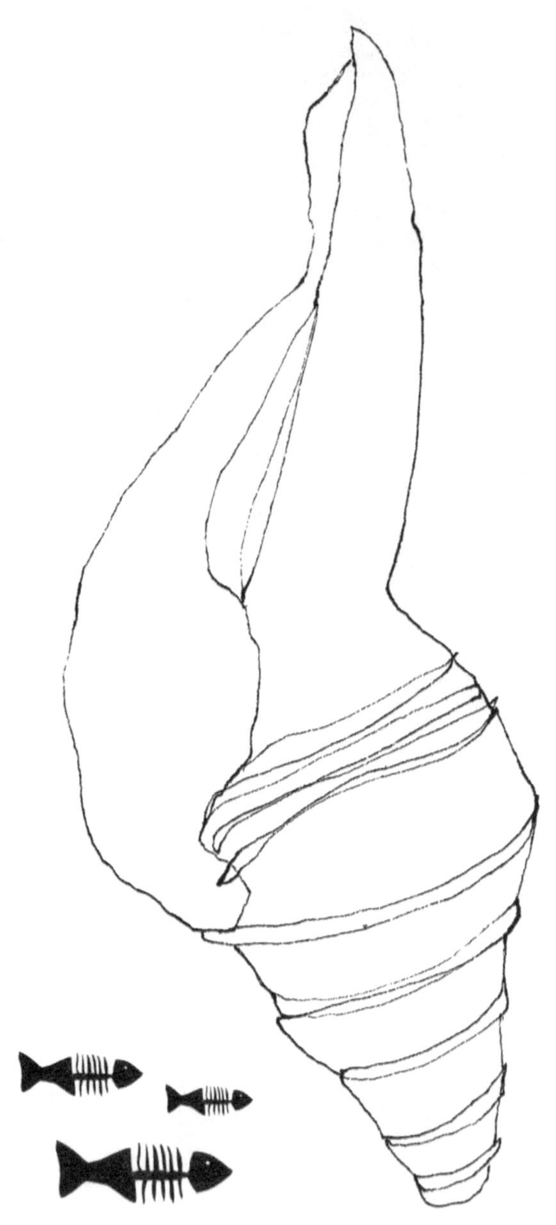

the word flees down a hole
paralysed for a moment looks into the hole

Distance is no more than a word

Thirst *is that word, sister of salt and sand and also, in its
unavoidable conclusion, the dried sister of silence*

Olvido García Valdés, Juan Eduardo Cirlot and Edmond Jabés

All is chance
the paper
and the wound that dwells
within but it needs
yes needs
an odd lamp—thirst

The butterfly comes back to the lamp
(…)

                                    and stays forever
among the things caught in its swing

José-Miguel Ullán and Eugenio Montale

LARA NOTEBOOK I
OR
JOURNEYS, LEAPS, STEPS AND
TRANSFORMATIONS FOR
UNE PETITE HISTOIRE

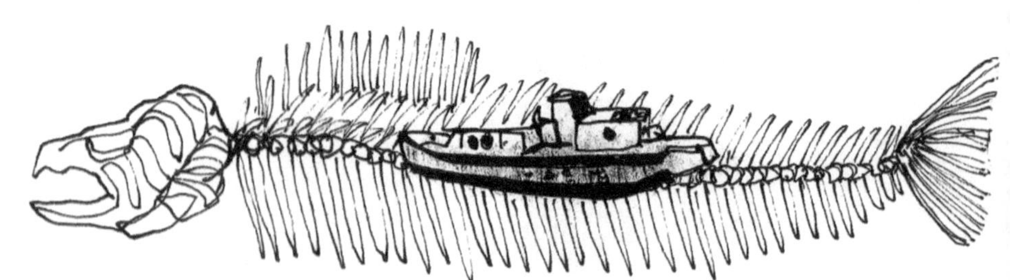

who writes waste
  paper if not me

    but yes
    my body the ladder *its* rungs of memory

—almost
          an assault

                        that which is
          un(re)cognised dawns sooner

    beyond

the threshold
          covered in leaves

to descend
to one bank
of the bridge
to the jumping-off point
or within
the *yes*

"a riverbank is unsown tomorrow

another embrace

near the chronicle   the sickle

she squashes bees with a fork   and now fear disem
                                                barks

and in my notebook honeystains and the cell bars

grow thicker

[i ask for Marco Polo
—i miss silk]

"you meld the wedding ring weight with the weight of ash
"we bear so many signs on our sunburnt shoulders

[every blank page brings us closer

to the b o o k where we will one day

                              find ourselves]

you cast your seed

                              names into the desert

          silent   erosion

                                   predict(s) me

sand among the sand cuts down
my traveller

who may not reach the root

of his *own* mirror

snake scar

      to be bridge or breast

—in the journey of the train
twisting my dormant animal—

skin is a trace

    :

     it polishes

sightlines_

      a journey   to wipe the walls from the *map*

           ^{to say love} like the ones who run away

    _rails   of a book yet to be opened

step by step we open the marrow
of the journey

and as we open ourselves.   we grow old

at the threshold of the forbidden
our hunger

        comes from a way away
and what remains

           is hidden

COWS AND FISH
OR
NOTEBOOK OF THE NEW SPECIES

what side of the light is truth —*not* that which
cuts or else all was
    its transformation   *or will not be*
                        LARA

swarm

tied to

the hive

vision

of all

our roots

there gather in the ponds
like little animals   salt on the tongue
of any

      dessication

it seeds where it has risen but it does not know
if it harvests or sows snail(s)hells
if it shares their hunger

                              ,seaweed reaper

complete furrows

                        forgets

in their alveoli grows

"the cotton wind captures

                        black birds

                              body
:st(amen)
              of sand

it splinters the lung
                where it dawns

with all the doors open apart

                              from the door

              that's closed and   *all the windows*

                              a beating
                    inside

              :wingbeat with phosphorus encrustations
on the wings

              it still resists like its watchtower
                              of dismembered
                              birds

a mollusc lives in the fisherman's scales—cyst
rehoused by the air
its soft body/ a spike. it sifts out pearls from sand/ signs
no net can catch and which will bite no hook

"if shame will let its tumour grow

hard flesh. dried udders. rocks that feed the un
known mother

the fish is a mammal that is a cow. it cuds comfort to
another cow which also ignores the word sea. maybe sea
is a word from semen. but empty/maybe sea is the limit of
the horizon at the point where it *burns* thirst

good to be hard flesh/ when you can walk over
a word without missing the fish

grey cement from the swing of things the child bursts
from the womb of ash.
its little transparency raises   [shrivelled arms / turned-in
hands/ disturbs the traverse of those signs]

because *there is another memory*
of the hook   to loosen
the knotted line

light before the secret
:
net
of half-open mouths

it does not
proforesee   metal
bitten by bone and which movement of this bough
will divine: *stitch through what is said*

"flesh forgets but not the illegible osseous   name

Lara Notebook II

PHOTO[N]GRAPHS
OR
NOTEBOOK OF FRACTURES
AND HOW TO HUNT GHOSTS WITH
  A HARPOON
AND OTHER WORDS THAT WOUND
  THE IMAGE
OR   AT
TEMPT IT *IF YOU CAN*

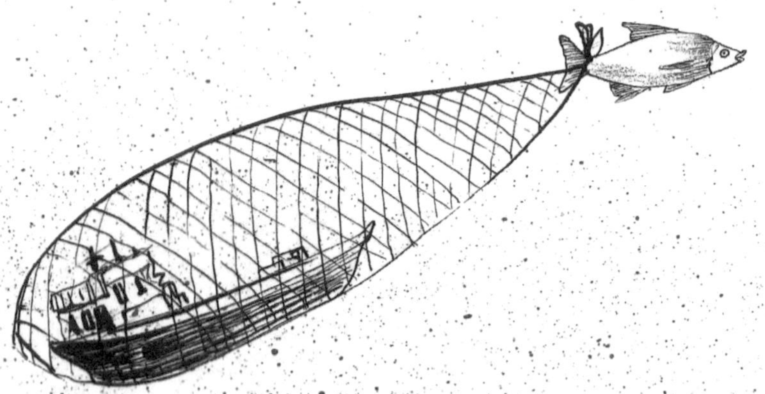

there is no desert to cross *when all is desert*

h o r i z o n bile   fossil   solar

this shore

                is too

                        close

under the river's silence there flows   another   river hurled

where there is too much si

               lens   and

the voice

       un
       hooks the image
    from memory

to look at

       how
   :
  from these
    waters

      these
   creatures

they see
      the
thirst
of earth
              the
thirst
to see
things

                        in
            the ankh
                    or of
            the page
                    which
misses

details

                    harpoon
              between two ab senses
                        :
                   t h i r s t

                   casting out faith
                                fully the hook
  as
     though
              there were no word   *or light*

                   to ar ti cu late ab senc es

                                    tremble
                        do it a gain

Lara Notebook I

and
unable
to speak of this desert as speech

moves

spreads

and dis
orders

its bones

flat land
bone
        nitrates
burn
now
unmarrowed.

                                dust is the
            b a c k b o n e
                                the burn
                clos
                ing

                                rust.

    :   skin p.aral.ysis
                                        and
                fishbones.

                                        it palps
    the
    burnt spot.

exodus

            striation   dead
                                       boats

     two umbilical   cords

                       boxed
boats run aground

                and silently
                     run
                        aground
in scars
    of salt
      the fishthorns.

ghosts.

                                        cotton
                        sailors.
ghosts.

This, the first English edition of *Aral*, was sent to the printer on 2 October, 2019, 140th anniversary of the birth of the American poet and insurance executive Wallace Stevens.

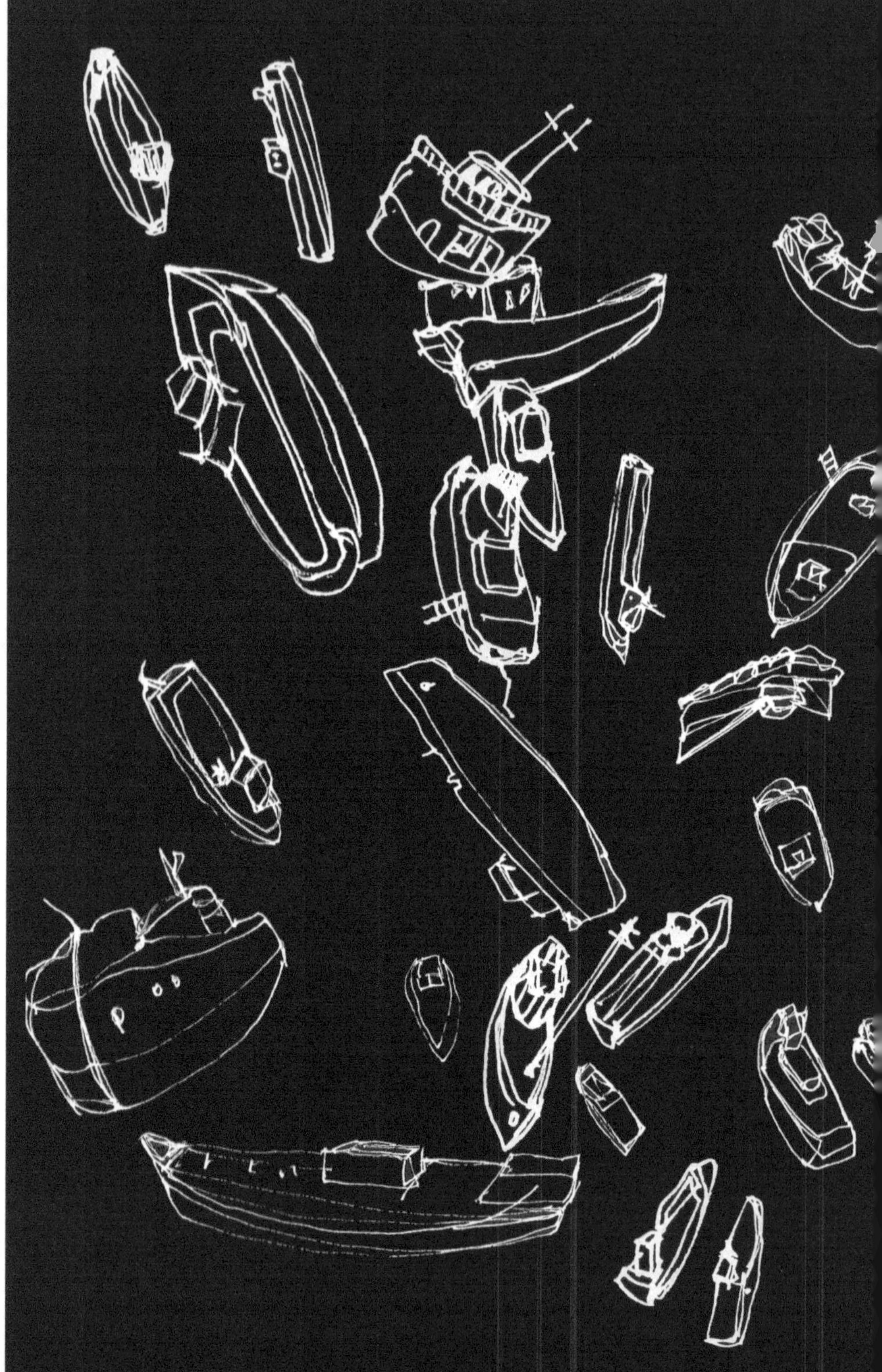

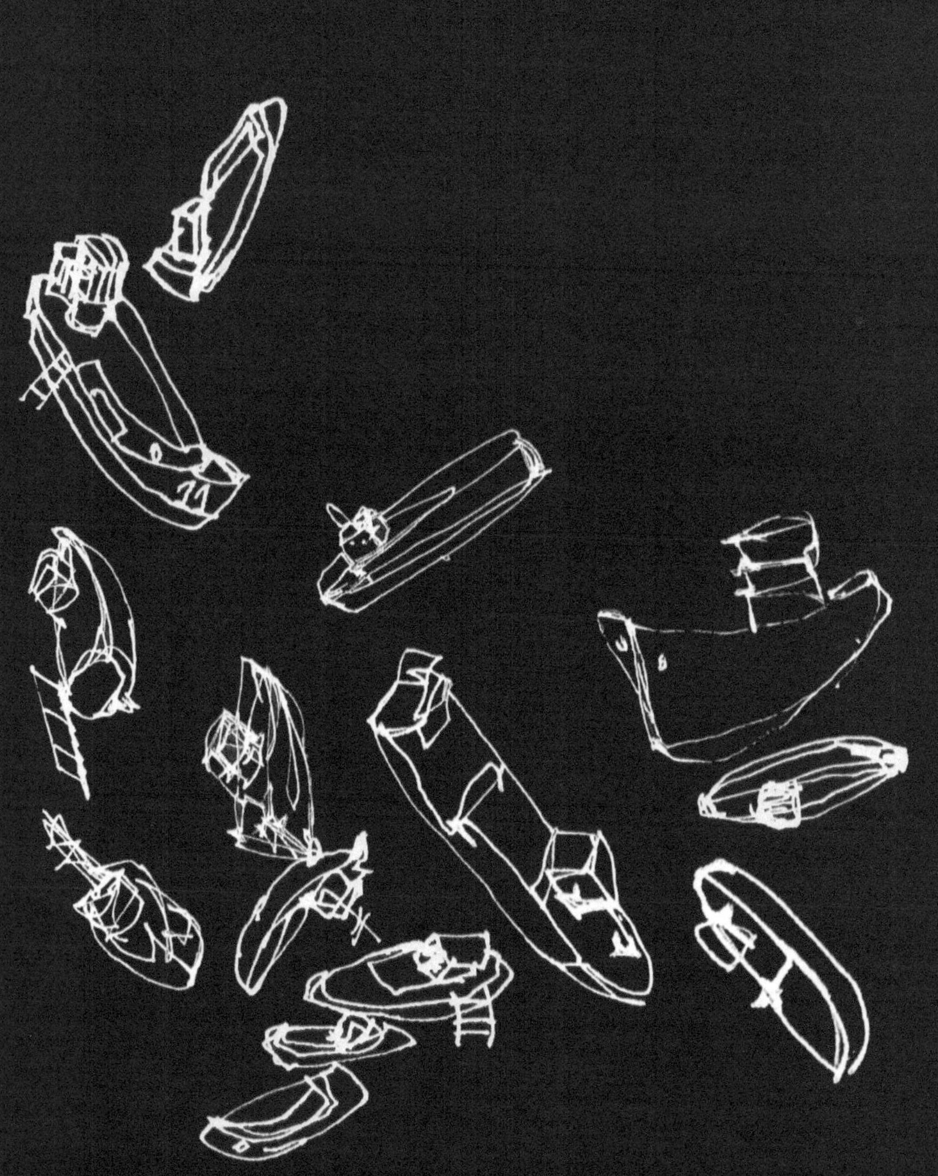